The Story of Lazarus

by

Rev. Bud Robinson

First Fruits Press
Wilmore, Kentucky
2015

The Story of Lazarus by Bud Robinson

Published by First Fruits Press, © 2015
Previously published by the Pentecostal Publishing Company, ©1909

ISBN: 9781621712008 (print), 9781621711995 (digital)

Digital version at
http://place.asburyseminary.edu/firstfruitsheritagematerial/96/

Robinson, Bud, 1860-1942.
    The story of Lazarus / by Bud Robinson.
    111 pages ; 21 cm.
    Wilmore, KY : First Fruits Press, ©2015.
    Reprint. Previously published: Louisville, KY : Pentecostal
    Publishing Company, ©1909.
    ISBN: 9781621712008 (pbk.)
    1. Lazarus, of Bethany, Saint -- Sermons. 2. Bible. N.T. --
    Biography. I. Title.
    BS2460.L3 R6 2015   244

Cover design by Amelia Hegle

First Fruits Press
The Academic Open Press of Asbury Theological Seminary
204 N. Lexington Ave., Wilmore, KY 40390
859-858-2236
first.fruits@asburyseminary.edu
asbury.to/firstfruits

The Story of Lazarus.

—BY—

BUD ROBINSON,

Author of "A Pitcher of Cream," "Walking With God Or the Devil, Which?" etc.

●━━●━━●━━●━━●

Thousand.

Pentecostal Publishing Company,
Louisville, Ky.

DEDICATION.

When I wrote my first book, Sunshine and Smiles, I lovingly dedicated it to the whole human family. What a poor, silly goose I was, for as I stood by the wayside with the book under my arm I cried to the passing throng, Ho! everyone that wants reading matter, come, buy Sunshine and Smiles with money, and the price is   but the whole human family seemed to pass me by like the wind and never even stopped to see what I had for sale; but I was not disheartened at all.

I went to work and wrote another book and called it A Pitcher of Cream, and I lovingly dedicated it to old Jessie, a lovely old Jersey cow which had been a good friend to me and my family. I told the reading public that there was no buttermilk or clabber, or blue-john or skimmed milk, in the book; but to my surprise old Jessie joined the Prohibition Party and voted the Prohibition ticket and went dry by a large majority; there I stood by the public highway with Sunshine and Smiles under one arm and A Pitcher of Cream under the other, with a grinning world on one side and a dry cow on the other. Ho! reader, reader, you must indeed be very stupid, to allow Sunshine and Smiles and A Pitcher of Cream to pass you by; but I have read that a fortune knocks at every man's door once in a lifetime and if he fails to open she goes on never to return.

As I have just completed the story of Lazarus, I lovingly dedicate this book to Miss Sallie, and if she doesn't beat the whole human family and old Jessie, I will be the worst deceived boy above ground.

CONTENTS:

THE AUTHOR'S PREFACE.

Dear Readers: I am not going to beg your pardon for sending out another book, but I am going to ask you to please overlook my mistakes and blunders, and be just as patient with me as you possibly can. I want to thank all of the dear brethren in the field who have given me any light and help on this remarkable man called Lazarus. I heard one sermon preached on Lazarus, by a Methodist pastor at Omaha, Ill., a few years ago; that is the only sermon I ever heard preached on Lazarus. I also read a little sketch in one of Dr. Carradine's books on Lazarus, but the man who gave me more help on Lazarus than any other man was Dr. McAmmons, a Methodist pastor in Chicago, Ill. Apart from these three men I never heard a man in my life say anything about Lazarus; but to me he is one of the most interesting characters that is discussed in the New Testament, and for the past three or four years I have been studying Lazarus as a type of the whole human family, and to my mind he comes nearer being a type of the whole human family than any other one character

that is found between the lids of the Bible.
There is no condition in life but what Lazarus
covers the ground. As a sick man he is a type
of the newborn babe with the carnal mind in its
heart, and as a dead man he is a type of the
child when it comes to the years of accountability, and chooses sin and dies, and is now
dead in trespasses and in sins; and as a bound
man he is a type of the child when he has gone
into sin and has been bound by the devil; as an
entombed man he is a type of the sinner when
he gives up all hope, and goes into the tomb of
despair; as a putrified man he is a type of
the old sinner when he becomes sin-hardened
and corrupted in his whole moral nature. Lazarus called out of the tomb is a type of the new
birth; Lazarus set free is a type of the experience of sanctification; Lazarus feasting with
his Lord is one of the most beautiful types of
the life of holiness that can be found in the old
Book; Lazarus persecuted by the high priest is
one of the most striking incidents in the life of
every holiness man. Just as sure as you get
sanctified you are sure to have the high priest
on your trail. It never fails. Just as sure as
you get filled with the Holy Ghost and go to
feasting with your Lord your testimonies will
stir up the carnal mind in the man that has not
got a clean heart, and he will become jealous

of you, and the fight will be on, O Christian soldier. Lazarus, the soul winner, is a beautiful type of the holiness evangelist of the present day. A Spirit-filled man is a soul winner. It is the natural order. It cannot be otherwise. It must be so in spite of men and devils.

BUD ROBINSON.

THE STORY OF LAZARUS.

CHAPTER I.

LAZARUS THE SICK MAN.

Lazarus is a type of the whole human family. No other man in the New Testament covers as much ground as the man Lazarus; he is a type of the sinner in every stage of life, and also a type of the Christian from the young convert to the old saint, as he passeth through the pearly gates into the beautiful city. The first mention that is made of Lazarus is in the eleventh chapter of St. John's gospel and the first verse. We read: "Now a certain man was sick named Lazarus."

The reader will notice that the first mention that is made of Lazarus is that he is a sick man. We read nothing of his parents; we suppose that he was an orphan boy. There is not one word about his mother or father in the New Testament. If he had a brother he is not referred to; we only hear of his two sisters, Mary and Martha. The first time that we hear of Lazarus he is sick. The Book says nothing of

his boyhood days, and, in fact, we hear but
little of Lazarus himself. We read nothing of
his standing in the community; not a word
about his education or his political or religious
views, but we suppose he was a very religious
man from the fact that the Master loved to go
to and abide in his little home in the village of
Bethany. This was one of the homes of the
Master, as He trod through the earth a homeless man in search of an opportunity to do
something for the other fellow. Bless His
dear name forever and ever. How I love Him
and how good He has been to me!

Now, in the first place Lazarus, as a sick
man, is the type of the newborn babe. When
the child is born into this world it comes to see
us with the carnal mind in its heart and is unwell morally. Lazarus was unwell physically
and the child is unwell spiritually, so the first
glimpse that we get of Lazarus and the newborn babe is that they are both unwell, and if
we will look at them for a few minutes we will
see that the disease proves fatal in each case.
We know that Lazarus died and if we will
look we will see that the child dies also. For
a little while let's take a look at the moral condition of the child and see if he isn't born into
this world with the disease of sin in him. We

will notice first Isaiah 1:2-6: "Hear, O heavens, and give ear, O earth: for the Lord has
spoken, I have nourished and brought up children, and they have rebelled against me.   The
ox knoweth his owner, and the ass his master's
crib: but Israel doth not know, my people doth
not consider.   Ah sinful nation, a people laden
with iniquity, a seed of evildoers, children that
are corrupters: they have forsaken the Lord,
they have provoked the Holy One of Israel,
unto   anger,   they   are   gone   away
backward.   Why   should   ye   be   strick-
en   any   more?   ye   will revolt   more and
more: the   whole   head   is   sick, and   the
whole heart is faint.   From the sole of the foot
even unto the head there is no soundness in it;
but wounds, and bruises, and putrifying sores:
they have not been closed, neither bound up,
neither mollified with ointment."

Now, reader, I submit to your honest judg-
ment the above description of the unregenerat-
ed human heart.   Does it not look like the
human family is in a depraved state?   If that is
not total depravity what would you call it?
They are put down below the ox and the ass,
two of the dullest dumb brutes in the field, and
they are both ahead of the children of Israel.
Oh, yes, my friend, the human family is born

with the old man in the heart and he begins his work as soon as the child is born; he doesn't wait until the child is grown to put him at the thing that he knows is contrary to the will of God; but as soon as the child is born the devil is ready to give him a job, and it is not long until he has him on the way to destruction.

I feel sure that King David wrote under the inspiration of the blessed Holy Ghost. See what he says about the child, Psalms 51:5: "Behold, I was shapen in iniquity; and in sin did my mother canceive me." Again, before we pass from the Psalmist, we will notice the 58th Psalm and the third verse: "The wicked are estranged from the womb: they go astray as soon as they be born, speaking lies." This doesn't look like they waited to be grown to go into sin. I have said it a number of times, and you may have said it before I ever thought of it, that every child that was ever born in Texas lied before it could talk and stole before it could walk. The Psalmist said that he was shapen in iniquity, and in sin did his mother conceive him. Well, that is the way they are all born into this world.

I have known children to be born into the homes of good, religious parents and these children were never conquered in their lives. I

have known some good Methodist mothers to
name their baby boy for one of the bishops and
consecrate him to the Lord to be made bishop,
and he was elected before he was two years
old.   You could go to the home and the two-
year-old boy was making all of the appoint-
ments; he commanded and his mother had to
obey; he screamed and whooped and yelled,
turned   over   chairs   and   slammed   the
doors,   and   would   get   up   and   throw
the teacups, and the knives and forks off
the table, and his mother and all of the other
children had to obey him or have one of the
biggest rackets that you have ever heard in all
of your life.   So you see, my friend, that Lazarus as a sick man is a pretty good representa-
tive of the child when it is born into the world
with the old man in its heart.   Lazarus was
sick and the child is not well by any means.

   Now for a little while we want to look at
some Scriptures over in the New Testament.
First, we want to look at the third verse of the
second chapter of Paul's letter to the Ephes-
ians, and just see for ourselves: "Among whom
also we all had our conversation in times past
in the lusts of our flesh, fulfilling the desires of
the flesh and of the mind; and were by nature
the children of wrath even as others."   The

apostle says here that we are by nature the children of wrath even as others. Notice first that he doesn't say we are the children of wrath by choice nor does he say that we are the children of wrath by practice; but notice what he does say; he says that we are the children of wrath by nature. Now reader, if you had a tree that was by nature a tree of wrath, what kind of fruit do you think would grow on it? Well, we can find out by going to Gallatians 5:19. Just see for yourself, and oh my, it almost takes your breath. "Now the works of the flesh are manifest, which the these: Adultery, fornication, uncleanness, lasciviousness, idolatry, witchcraft, hatred, varience, emulations, wrath, strife, seditions, heresies, envyings, murders, drunkenness, revellings, and such like." I submit to your intelligence as an honest man or woman, don't you think that the above crowd is in a state of total, yes in a state of teetotal depravity. That crowd of people is qualified to commit any sin that is known to the human family, and yet I have heard much about our beautiful human nature; but just look children and see for yourself. I don't suppose that a man could find a harder crowd this side of the pit than the above.

But before we leave Paul's letter to the

Galatians, we want to notice the 17th verse of the 5th chapter: "For the flesh lusteth against the Spirit, and the Spirit against the flesh: and these are contrary the one to the other: so that ye cannot do the things that ye would."   The reader will notice here that the word flesh refers to the carnal mind, or the old man or inbred sin, whichever you would rather call it. Of course the word flesh there could not refer to your bones and blood, for the Spirit of God and your bones could not be contrary the one to the other; but there is something in man that is contrary to the Spirit of God, and of course it is the carnal mind, for St. Paul says in Romans 8:7 that, "Because the carnal mind is enmity against God: for it is not subject to the law of God, neither indeed can be."   So you see at a glance that Romans 8:7 explains Gal. 5:17, where Paul says that the flesh lusteth against the Spirit and the Spirit against the flesh; for these are contrary the one to the other, so that ye cannot do the things that ye would.   If the child doesn't bring the carnal mind into this world with him when he is born of the flesh, then he must receive it when he is born of the Spirit, and you could not think of a thing of that kind.   But at the same time we see a man here with two minds in him and each one wants to rule and each one wants to sit on the throne and hold the reins of your life and do the driving.

Now reader, the only way to make these Scriptures plain is to see them in their true light. The child is born into the world with the carnal mind in him and when he is born of the Spirit he receives the spiritual mind; he already had the carnal mind and now he becomes a double-minded man, both carnal and spiritual, and the war is between the carnal mind and the spiritual mind. When we are born of the Spirit we receive the spiritual mind and when we are baptized with the Holy Ghost and fire we get rid of the carnal mind and that leaves the mind of Christ in our heart to reign without a rival. If you will look, you will see that Lazarus as a sick man is a type of the child that is born into this world with the old man in its heart and if you are not satisfied with the above Scriptures, at your leisure you might read St. Mark 7:21, 22, and when you get through with that lesson you might read Romans 3:10-20. By that time you will be convinced that the human family is born out of gear and out of harmony with God, out of harmony with itself, and out of harmony with the world round about it.

Is it not a fact that two old sinners can't hardly live in the same community, and get along with each other; sometimes they don't do it, but fall out and fight and go to law with each other. Again I have seen boys not ten years old meet and fight every Sunday for nearly a year and almost kill each other, and nobody think anything of it at all. Again I have seen small children two or three years old fall out and fight just like beasts, and I have seen their mothers pull them apart and whip them and it seemed to do no good. Now the question naturally arises in the mind of a fellow if the child is not a depraved being, what is the matter with it? Don't you see a sick Lazarus there, and don't you see that the disease has proven fatal and that Lazarus is dangerously ill?

CHAPTER II.

LAZARUS, THE DEAD MAN.

Now, reader, for sometime we have been looking at Lazarus, the sick man, but now we have come to the second stage in the history of this remarkable man. Just as truly as Lazarus the sick man is a type of the child that is born into the world with the carnal mind in its heart, Lazarus, the dead man, is a type of the child when it comes to the years of accountability, and chooses sin and dies; and now the child is dead in trespasses and in sins; and just as truly as Lazarus was dead physically the child is dead spiritually, or morally. As you look at Lazarus you don't see a sick man, you see a dead man; and as you look at your boy you don't see a child with only the carnal mind in him, you see a sinner dead in trespasses and in sins. The teaching of the old Book i that the sinner is dead. We first saw the child a sinner by nature, and now we have before us a sinner by choice; quite a difference. So you see the child chose sin and died.

We read in Romans 7:8, "That being dead

wherein we were held." That is a picture of a
dead man bound by death. What an awful
thought! A double death it seems. Again in
Romans 7:11 we read, "For sin, taking occasion by the commandment, deceived me, and
by it slew me." You see the thing put the man
to death. It slew him. What was it that slew
him? Well, he says that it was sin. When
did it slay him? Just at the same time that it
slew you. When he came to the years of accountability and chose sin,he died,morally, ;now
he is dead—not a sick man, but a dead man.
He was not dead physically or he could not
have written this letter; he was dead spiritually,
and sin, the old man, killed him just like he has
all the rest of the human family.

We read again in Eph. 2:1, 2: "And you
hath he quickened, who were dead in trespasses
and sins; wherein in time past ye walked according to the course of this world, according
to the prince of the power of the air, the spirit
that now worketh in the children of disobed-
dence." Reader, just see what all the apostle
says about these people: First, they were dead,
and they were dead in sins. That proves that
they had died somewhere back down their
trail, and he said that in time past they had
walked according to the course of this world.

He also said that they had walked according to the prince of the power of the air, and that these children had in them the spirit of disobedience. What was that spirit of disobedience? Nothing more or less than the old man or the carnal mind, or the indwelling sin, as Paul calls it, or the old Adam, or the roots of bitterness, as he calls it in another place in the old Book.

Now we will turn to Paul's letter to the Colossians and read the thirteenth verse of the second chapter. Notice what he says: "And you being dead in your sins and the uncircumcision of your flesh, hath he quickened together with him, having forgiven you all trespasses." In this text we have before us a dead man, and then we see him quickened, or made alive, which proves that the man was dead. You see a dead Lazarus and a dead sinner. Lazarus was dead physically and the sinner is dead spiritually. One is without physical life and the other is without spiritual life. The sinner is as bad off spiritually as Lazarus is physically; there is no difference in them. If Lazarus ever gets out of that grave there will have to be a miracle performed, for he is a dead man; and if that sinner ever gets out of that grave of spiritual death there will have to be a miracle

performed, for he is a dead man—just as dead
spiritually as Lazarus was physically. He is
dead to God and to holines, to righteousness,
eternal life, and to all that is good and pure;
and he is alive to all that is bad. What a pity.
Oh my, how many I have seen just like that.

Now in I Tim. 5:6 we read: "But she that
liveth in pleasure is dead while she liveth."
There is the picture of a worldly woman, a so-
ciety-runner, a pleasure-seeker, a fun-lover, a
God-forgetter, a Christ-despiser, and a blood-
rejecter. Paul says that she is dead. Yes, and
so was Lazarus; so you see that the type still
holds good. She is alive to everything that be-
longs to this world; she is alive socially, she is
alive mentally, and she is alive financially;
she is only dead to her eternal welfare. What
an awful thought; dead to eternal life and alive
to eternal death! Somebody may say poor
Lazarus. Yes, and somebody ought to say
poor woman; she is as bad off as Lazarus ever
was. How could she be in a worse fix than
she is in? Paul says that she is dead while she
liveth, and so was I and so were you, my
friend.

There is nothing beautiful about death;
nothing lovely, nothing that looks encouraging
or hopeful. If it were not for the fact that our

blessed Christ has promised us a glorious resurrection, I don't see how I ever could bear the thought of going down to the grave for it makes my very blood run cold when I think of the grave. If it is my Father's will, I would rather preach holiness until Jesus comes and then go up with Him and not go by the grave at all, but I may have it to do, as my brethren have had to do.

CHAPTER III.

LAZARUS, THE BOUND MAN.

Now, reader, we have noticed Lazarus the sick man a type of the child born into the world with the carnal mind in it, and we have noticed Lazarus the dead man a type of the child when it comes to the years of accountability and chooses sin and dies and becomes dead in trespasses and in sins. Now we have before us Lazarus, the bound man. We see from the case of Lazarus that it was the custom in the Oriental world to bind a corpse when they got it ready for burial. Just why they would bind a dead man is a mystery to me. It doesn't look reasonable, but we see that it was done. It may be possible that the Lord allowed them to do it in order to teach us some spiritual lessons that would be profitable to us in our day, for we know that sin will not only kill the man but we know that it will bind him after he is dead.

Just as truly as Lazarus was bound the sinners in our country are bound also. We read that Lazarus was bound hand and foot, and we

see that the sinners of our day are bound hand
and foot also.   Lazarus was helpless and the
sinners are helpless.   Lazarus had no power to
deliver himself from the cords that were around
him, and the sinner has no power to deliver
himself from the cords that the devil has put
around him.   We read in Psalms 107:10:
"Such as sit in darkness and in the shadow of
death,   being bound in affliction and iron."
That, of course, is the picture of the sinner as
King David saw him and he says that the fellow is bound in affliction and iron.   In the next
verse he tells us why the fellow was bound. He
says it was "Because he had rebelled against
the words of God, and contemned the counsel
of the most High."   How much like the twentieth century sinners that is.   You can see them
if you will look.

Now reader, we want to read a verse in 2
Tim. 2:26: "And that they may recover themselves out of the devil, who are taken captive
by him at his will." You will notice that somebody here is described as being in the snare of
the devil, and not only in his snare but taken
by him captive at his will, and don't you see
that if the devil has a fellow in his snare and
is taking him captive at his will, that
he has the fellow bound?   How could

he take him captive if the fellow was not bound by the devil? Of course you know that you meet sinners every day that are as completely bound by the devil as they would be if they had chains on them. I have seen sinners that were afraid to try to escape from the devil, they were so completely overpowered by him. I have heard people say, How does the devil bind a fellow? Well, he begins by first putting the carnal mind in the human heart, and the child is born with depravity in its heart. The carnal mind leads him astray and he chooses sin, and now he is dead in trespasses and in sins. After he is dead morally the devil begins to put the cords on him and bind him. One of the first cords that the devil puts on him is the cord of disobedience. Two or three years ago you had a sweet baby, but to-day you have a stubborn, hard-headed disobedient boy. You are surprised to see him as stubborn as he is and wonder who he takes it after. The next thing you know, your boy is a profane swearer and it almost breaks your heart, but the devil has put another cord on him. Don't you see Lazarus bound and don't you see your own son bound also?

The next string that the devil puts on him will be tobacco; now he is a cigarette fiend and will smoke and lie about it, and tell his mother that he never smoked in his life. When she catches up with him and he has to own up he will get mad and swear right in the presence of his old mother, and she is afraid to say a word. He begins to threaten to leave home if he can't have his way, and his mother thinks it is all because he has been keeping bad company. Well, of course, he has. The devil has been after him ever since he was born and is still on his trail; and the devil may take that nice boy of yours and put him in the chain gang, and finally in the state prison, and finally in an awful hell.

Don't you see that the young man is bound by the devil and led by him captive at his will? When your boy was a babe and kicked and screamed and fought and bit and turned over chairs and threw things off the table, it was so funny that everybody laughed at him, and even his mother thought it was cute in the little fellow. When he takes one of his spells now it is not as funny as it used to be. His mother sits down and weeps by the hour. What is the trouble now? Well, Lazarus is dead and they have bound him for the burial and his friends are weeping over him. Your babe is no longer a smiling babe; he is a great rough sin-

ner and bound by the cords of disobedience,
profanity, tobacco, strong drink, Sabbath des-
ecration, lust and anger; and many of them
are bound by the cords of theft and murder.
Oh my, how different he looks now to what he
did before the devil put the cords around him!
You see, reader, that the devil laid his plans
in the garden, and he is working out his plans
in the field. Yes, in the fields of life. How
busy he is; not a moment to lose. His victims
are driven by him just like they were beasts.

Again the devil not only has power to bind
the souls of men but he seems to have power
to bind their bodies. In proof of that fact I
offer you the following Scriptures: Look at
Luke's gospel, 13:16: "And ought not this
woman, being a daughter of Abraham, whom
Satan hath bound, lo, these eighteen years, be
loosed from this bond on the Sabbath day?"
The Master Himself said that this woman was
the daughter of Abraham, and He also said that
Satan had her bound for eighteen years. How
many have I seen that Satan had bound and
put them on their beds of affliction. I have seen
them all over the United States as completely
bound by Satan physically as they were morally. He is an awful devil and he hates Christ
and wants to defeat Him and he wants to rule

this country. I have seen some people that I think the devil knew he never would get their souls and he seemed to afflict their bodies to hinder their life's work. I as much believe the devil tried for years to kill me as I believe that I am alive to-day.

Now we will turn and read Acts 10:38: "How God anointed Jesus of Nazareth with the Holy Ghost and with power; went about doing good, and healing all that were oppressed of the devil; for God was with him." Here the reader will notice that Jesus was to heal all that were oppressed of the devil, so we see that he (the devil), had power to bind a woman for eighteen years and here he has power to oppress or to afflict mankind. We also see that Jesus had power to heal all that were oppressed of the devil, for God was with Him. You may take a man or a woman that has a fine mind and a fine, strong body, and a soul all on fire for God, and they can do much to the kingdom of the devil; he knows it as well as we do and he hates such people.

I will only speak of one other case of binding, and that is the case of the man in the tombs recorded in the eighth chapter of Matthew, the fifth chapter of Mark, and the eighth chapter of Luke. Saint Mark says of this man that, no man could bind him; Saint Luke says that he was driven of the devil. Mark you, he doesn't say that he was led or tolled of the devil, but that he was driven of the devil. They also tell us that he wore no clothes, that he made his dwellings among the tombs and that he cut himself with the stones. There was a man that the devil had bound mentally, morally and physically, and if it had not been for the fact that Jesus of Nazareth went by that man would have stayed in that awful condition until the day of his death. What would we do without a Savior? Just think of a world with a devil in it and no Christ in it. If we did not have the Holy Spirit in the world to restrain and check and drive back the devil, what is it that he would not do? My, man, it almost makes your blood freeze in your veins to think of living in a world without a Savior in it. I believe that the sinners of the country are restrained by the grace of God, and while they may not know it, yet I believe it is true, and we cannot tell what they would do if it were not for the grace of God. Just look at the man in the tombs and you have the human family under the dominion of the devil instead of under the dominion of the Son of God. Now, reader, if you can see one ray of hope there I wish you would show it to me, for I am frank to say that the picture is as black as the midnight hour to me.   When I see men and women going on in sin and rejecting the Savior I wonder if they want to go to the tombs.

CHAPTER IV.

LAZARUS, THE ENTOMBED MAN.

We have come to the fourth chapter of the history of this remarkable man and we have seen Lazarus, the sick man, Lazarus, the dead man, Lazarus, the bound man, and now we have before us Lazarus, the entombed man. Just think of it—sick, dead, bound and buried —a type of the lost and ruined sinner. Lazarus, the sick man, is a type of the child that is born with the carnal mind in its heart. Lazarus, the dead man, is a type of the child when it comes to the years of accountability and chooses sin and dies and becomes dead in trespasses and in sins. Lazarus, the bound man, is a type of the child when it goes into a life of sin and is bound by its habits and the devil leads him captive at his will; and now, Lazarus, in the tomb, is the type of every sinner when he gives up all hope as you have seen them. Oh my, I have seen sinners by the thousands give up all hope and go into the tomb of despondency, and, spiritually speaking, they were as much in the tomb spiritually as Lazarus was physically. All hope was gone and at a glance you could see that they had gone into the tomb of despair; and if a lowly Nazarene doesn't come by and call them out they will stay there forever and forever. The land is loaded down with men and women who used to have hope and the devil has swept them off their feet so often that today they are in the tomb of despair and every hope has fled, every friend is dead;they have an empty purse, an aching head, and an empty stomach, with no Christ, no God, no salvation, and no hope of heaven. Where are they to-day? Oh, my friend, you can answer in the tomb of despair. Look at them and hear their sad wail as they march through this world without one ray of hope, homeless, friendless, and penniless, without one ray of sunshine over their door.

You remember when Lazarus went into the tomb Mary and Martha lost all hope, and when Jesus appeared on the scene their hopes were as completely buried as Lazarus was, and there are millions to-day with every hope in the tomb. The burial has already taken place, and despondency has settled down over them and they are ready to-day to take their own lives. They are doing it by the tens of thousands. Why do they do such a thing? somebody may ask. Because they have given up all hope, and when hope goes there is nothing to build on. But, somebody may ask, why don't they get up and get a move on them? Well, just simply because a dead man can't get up, a blind man can't see, a dead man can't hear, a bound man can't walk, the man in the tomb is a hopeless man, and so we can just make up our mind that if a Christ doesn't come along, Lazarus will never get out of the tomb, and the sinner will never awake out of his dead state of guilt and condemnation. I have known some men to be converted and start off well and run for a while and then the devil would sweep them off their feet. In a few months they would get reclaimed and make a fresh start and run pretty well for a while and finally backslide again; the next time it was several years before you could get them to make another start but their friends would plead with them and pray for them and by and by they would make another start and run for a while, and to their surprise they find the same old enemy in their heart; as they struggle with it they almost give up hope and finally go to their pastor and consult with him and ask him if they can be delivered from that awful uprising in their breast. He tells them that they cannot;

that he, himself, has the same kind of struggles that they have; that there is no remedy and, that if they will be faithful till death the Lord will give them a crown of life.

While they fight the beast on the inside the devil laughs at them and tells them that they had just as well give it up at once and be done with it forever, and about this time he comes up to the fellow and tells him he had just as well take a dram, for he can't hold out anyhow and the poor fellow yields to the tempter and gets on another big drunk.   When he sobers up and sees his condition he gives up all hope and goes down into the tomb of despair, and he is as much in the tomb as Lazarus was.   He was sick, he died; he was bound, he went into the tomb of despair, and there he will stay until some outside power calls him out.

Again I have met people, by the tens of thousands, who, at one time hoped to be well off some day and they have fought poverty and low wages and high prices and their hardships bravely, and each year they have run behind a little and maybe could not pay their bills; they would almost give up all hope, but they would take fresh courage and buckle down to it a little harder and think that they would come out ahead next year.   Sure, but to their surprise

the next year they were further behind than
they were the year before, and finally they
gave up all hope of ever owning a home of
their own, and they have settled down to the
idea of living in a little rented cabin all the
days of their lives. To-day their names are
legion that have given up all hope of ever being anything but a cheap day laborer. Their
wives are half dressed, their children are uned-
ucated, and they are American white slaves
and their hopes are in the tomb. Their prospects in life are as completely buried as Lazarus was.

Again, I have seen people who were on their
beds of affliction and for weeks and months and
maybe for years they were in great hopes of
some day being well; they fought pain and suf-
fering with a brave heart. In the face of afflictions they would see themselves well and out in
the fields, in the woods, on the creeks, and on
the mountains, as they used to be. They hear
of a great medicine that is supposed to cure all
diseases that are known to the human family,
and of course they send for it and take it according to directions. To their sad surprise
they get no relief, and then they hear of something else that cures all of the human ills. They
send for that and take it in great hopes of soon

being well again, but find no relief whatever, and after a while hope, that blessed hope the stay of life, takes its everlasting flight, and to-day they are on their beds by the tens of thousands and they never expect to get off of that ded until they go into their box. All hopes have gone into the tomb and they are as completely entombed as Lazarus was.   No more of this world's pleasure for that man; no more days out in the beautiful sunshine;   no more days to sit out on the porch and feel the soft wind play on his withered cheek; no more days to spend at the house of God; that poor man is bound by the cords of afflictions and he is in the tomb of despair. Every hope has left the country where that man lives.   Yonder he lies on his couch, helpless and hopeless, so far as this world is concerned, and he may be friendless and homeless and penniless also.   Thousands of them are, and they lie in the hospital up and down the land by the thousands.   How sad!

CHAPTER V.

LAZARUS, THE PUTRIFIED MAN.

We now have before us Lazarus, the putrified man, and in this stage he represents the old sinner in the last stage of sin just before he drops into the pit of eternal despair. We have seen him first, a sick man, second, a dead man, third, a bound man, fourth, the entombed man, and fifth, a putrified man. These are the five steps in the life of the sinner, from the crowing babe with the carnal mind in its heart, to the old sinner, reeking in sin and vice and dropping into the pit.

The reader will notice that there is no physical soundness left in Lazarus; he has corrupted throughout—no soundness at all left in him, and when the old sinner comes to the last stage of life he has corrupted throughout and there is no moral soundness left in him. He is now qualified and prepared by the devil to commit any crime that is known to the human family, and anything that the devil will dictate, he will do. He is as corrupt morally as Lazarus was physical-

ly. I know some may draw back and say that
I have overdrawn the picture, but I feel that I
have not in the least, and for a few minutes let's
look at Isaiah 1:6, and see what the old prophet says about man in his last stage: "From
the sole of the foot even unto the head there is
no soundness in it; but wounds, and bruises,
and putrifying sores; they have not been closed,
neither bound up, neither mollified with ointment."

Now reader, don't you see that the old sinner is in the same condition, morally, that Lazarus was physically? You just think of a man
full of wounds and bruises and putrifying sores
and of course it has reference to his moral condition, and not his physical condition, for no
man could live if his physical man were in the
condition that is described in the above text.
But just look at the man as he walks the streets
of the city, and you will see the saloon, the
gambling house, the race track, the ballroom,
the theatre, the circus, bawdy house, the cala-
boose, the county jail, the state prison, the gallows, a broken heart, and a wrecked life, a
ruined home, a lost soul, and the grave of the
drunkard.

The old Book says that the child of God is
to grow in grace and in the knowledge of our

Lord and Savior Jesus Christ; but the same
Book says of the sinner that the last stage of
that man is worse than the first. Don't you see
Lazarus in all of the different stages in which
we have followed him? When Lazarus first
died you could wash and dress him and shave
him and put a new suit of clothes on him, and
pin a bouquet of lovely flowers on him, and he
looked nice and respectable after he was dead;
and so did your boy. After your boy chose sin
and died he could hold a cigarette between his
thumb and fore-finger, and draw the smoke
down into his lungs and blow out through his
nose, and some people thought that he was
alive; but from the standpoint of morality he
was as dead as Lazarus was physically.

Again, when you look at Lazarus now you
see a man that you can't handle. There was a
time when you could handle Lazarus, but it is
not now. He says to you, Hands off, gentle-
men, without saying a word to you, and you
obey him and keep your hands off of him.
Well, why can't we handle him now? somebody may say. Because he has putrified, and
that means hands off. How much like your
son that is. When your boy first went into sin,
you could handle him pretty well and he seemed to have some sound streaks left in him, but

just look at him now. He says, Hands off,
mother, and she has to obey him. You see
that just after he went into sin he seemed to
have some respect and some regard for the will
and wish of his mother, but not so to-day. See,
his manhood and money and health and friends
are gone, and he is called by some people a
bum, by others a jail bird and by others a
criminal. He is now growing in sin and the
knowledge of the devil and is making his last
run for the pit and outer darkness.

He is now a graduate from the school of sin
and holds in his possession a diploma signed
by the devil. On the face of his diploma the
devil himself says of this man that, he is qualified to commit any crime that is known to the
human family; he further says of this man that
he has no time to waste on old men and women
and if you can't make him up a class of boys
and girls that he will have to go on to the next
village, for his time is precious and that he
must catch the youths of the land before they
get their eyes open; that he is prepared to teach
all youths the latest arts in any line of sin that
they may choose; that if you don't think that he
can commit the blackest and most devilish
crimes that are known to the human family, all
he asks is that you give him one chance only.

and if he doesn't convince the most skeptical mind of his ability to commit crime then he will give it up.   That is a fair proposition of its kind, but the man is indeed stupid that would deny the above statement of the devil.   Think of an American woman that would persuade her husband to have his life heavily insured and when all of the papers are fixed up and made payable to her at his death she slips into the room while he is asleep and with his own razor cuts him to pieces, cutting him seventeen times in the face and neck and over the heart until she sees him struggle to death in his own blood. I was in the city when the trial was going on, Of course any thinking man knows that the scheme was hatched out in the pit, and was among the first brood that the devil hatched off.

Somebody might say, why on earth would a woman do such a thing?   Well, don't you see that Lazarus has putrified?   Don't you see that that woman was as corrupt morally as Lazarus was physically?   Don't you see how ghastly Lazarus looks?   Just turn and look at that old sinner as he goes down town to his trial.   He has committed some crime and the officers are on the way to jail and to trial with him.

Matthew, Mark and Luke all describe a fel- low that stayed out in the tombs. Now this fel-

low that is on trial here in the city stays down
in the slums, and is a slum runner when he is
out of jail.   You can look at the fellow and
see he was born with the carnal mind in him;
that his disease proved fatal, that he died, that
he was bound, that he then went into the tomb
of despair and that he has now putrified and
is as corrupt morally as Lazarus was physically.

We have now covered the five stages of sin
and the five stages that we have seen Lazarus
in are a type of the sinner from the day of his
birth until the day of his death.   You see Lazarus sick, dead, bound, buried, and putrified,
and you see the sinner in all of the above con-
ditions, from the screaming child to the old sinner with the rope around his neck, as he was
swung off of the gallows and went out into
eternal despair without one ray of hope.

CHAPTER VI.

THE FIRST RAY OF HOPE.

Now, reader, we come to the first ray of hope as we discuss the history of this remarkable man. What was it? Well, look and see for yourself. Jesus, who is the hope of the world, appears on the scene, and when Christ comes to a world, or to a city, or a village, or to a single individual, they can never be the same again. From the night that the angel band swung low in the heavens and the shepherds heard them sing, Peace on earth and good will toward men, the world has never been the same, and can never be the same, for a Savior has come, and thank God has called for us, and there has been new hope and new desires and new expectations, and new prospects, and our up-look from that night until to-day as a world has been all that was needed; and when we look at that thing that we call future we see a Savior before we see the other end, and then we sing, "There will be no dark valley when Jesus comes, to gather His loved ones home." As Christ was the first ray of hope to this dark sin-cursed world so is He the first ray of hope to the poor, lost sinner for He is the light of the world.

When Christ appeared in the little village of Bethany four days after the death of Lazarus, there was a ray of hope that settled down over the village, and he had no sooner reached the village than Martha was out to meet Him. When she saw Him she told Him at once that if He had been there her brother had not died. That shows the confidence and the faith that she had in Him although everything goes to prove that she had no idea on earth that Lazarus would ever be resurrected until the end of time. Such a thing, that Lazarus would be resurrected that day, was undreamed of with her. It seemed to be enough for Martha just to know that the Master had come, and when she had unburdened her heart to the Lord she seemed to think that something was going to happen, though she did not know just what it was. As the burden rolled away from her own heart, she at once turned and ran for Mary and said to her, The Master has come and calleth for thee, and we read that Mary arose and went to the place where Jesus was. He had not yet come into the village, and you can see her as she hastens through the village to meet Him; when she met Him she fell down at His feet saying, Lord, if thou hadst been here my brother had not died.

Now, reader, you can see at a glance that neither of these girls had any idea of what the visit of the Master had in store for them. Their poor hearts had been buried with Lazarus, or, in other words, their hopes had. How many times in my meetings have I heard mothers raise a shout because a wayward son had heard the voice of the Son of God and was coming home. I say thanks be unto God for a Christ that will visit a community, lift heavy burdens, comfort sad hearts, lift up the downtrodden, revive the drooping spirits, speak peace to the troubled soul, and revive the hopes of those in despair. And as our blessed Savior walked into the little village of Bethany you can hear Him say, Lift up your heads oh ye gates, and be ye lifted up ye everlasting doors, and the King of glory shall come in. Now just think of the honor of having the blessed Son of God to visit our town or village. Would we ever get over it? Just think of you and Jesus walking the streets of your own town together. The first thing He did when He got to Bethany was to comfort the broken-hearted. Well, the old Book says of Him that He went about

doing good and healing all that were oppressed
of the devil, for God was with Him. We read
of Him in Isaiah, 61:1-3: "The Spirit of the
Lord God is upon me; because the Lord hath
anointed me to preach good tidings unto the
meek; he hath sent me to bind up the broken-
hearted, to proclaim liberty to the captives, and
the opening of the prison to them that are
bound; to proclaim the acceptable year of the
Lord, and the day of vengeance of our God; to
comfort all that mourn; to appoint unto them
that mourn in Zion, to give unto them beauty
for ashes, the oil of joy for mourning, the garment of praise for the spirit of heaviness; that
they might be called trees of righteousness, the
planting of the Lord, that he might be glorified."   It seems like the above Scripture was
written for the little family at Bethany.

We see that Mary and Martha are to be
comforted and that their broken hearts are to be
bound up and that Christ is to pour in the oil
of joy and to give them beauty for ashes, and
the garment of praise for the spirit of heaviness;
and as Lazarus was dead and in the prison of
death he was to be set free. You see death
had taken him captive and bound him and put
him in the tomb of death and Christ said that
He was to open the prison to them that were

bound.   We thank God that when Christ arrived in Bethany, One was there who could handle death.   So, dear sinner, there is hope, if the Son of God will only come into the community.   Bless His name for the thought that He ever came into the settlement where I lived. I will never let Him hear the last of it, for I, like Lazarus, was a dead man and a bound man and in the tomb and putrified and hopelessly lost, but now I live.   Glory to God!

CHAPTER VII.

CHRIST, THE RESURRECTION.

In our last chapter we had the first ray of hope and in this one we have Christ, the resurrection and the life. You see that there is not only hope, but thank God there is help and not only help, but there is help at hand, for you can see at a glance that if Christ can't do something supernatural there is no use in His going to Bethany, for the man there is dead. You see that Lazarus is beyond turning a new leaf or making new resolutions for he is cold and stiff in the arms of death, but Christ is in the village and has already declared Himself to be the resurrection and the life. This statement from the lips of the blessed Son of God gave these heart-broken girls a double hope, and so it does us. How gloomy the grave would look if it were not for the statement of the blessed Son of God, that He was the resurrection and the life.

He proved His doctrine to be true before night. The grave has no terror for a fully saved man and for proof of that fact you go to

a big camp meeting and just listen to the holy
people testify, sing and shout and
see them dance before the Lord, just as if there
was not a grave on all the face of the earth.
The holy people are not looking down at a
hole in the ground, they are looking above the
clouds and shouting, and when they do look
at the grave they only look at it as a kind of a
gateway to something better.   The apostle
Paul said, Oh death, where is thy sting, oh
grave, where is thy victory.   Some fifteen hun-
dred years before the sad day in Bethany Job
had asked a question and it was this: "If a man
die shall he live again?" and the question had
never been answered and could not be answered until it was answered by the blessed Son
of God.   When He went into Bethany and
said I am the resurrection and the life, a new
doctrine had been borne to the world and a
new hope had sprung up in the hearts of the
little family at Bethany and from that day to
the present the doctrine of the resurrection has
been settled in the minds of all true believers,
for if there be no resurrection of the dead, says
the Apostle Paul, then is our preaching vain,
and your faith is also vain.   Then he adds, ye
are yet in your sins, if the dead rise not.
     All Bible Christians believe that when a

sinner repents God pardons him; that when a
believer consecrates, God sanctifies him; that
when a saint is resurrected God glorifies him;
The sinner is resurrected from the state of
moral death when he is converted, and the believer is purified from a state of carnality when
he is sanctified, and the saint is resurrected from
a state of physical death when he is glorified.
There is nothing hard about that to a man that
believes the Bible and is on his way to a home
in the glory land.

Now just at this moment Christ walks up
and declares Himself to be the resurrection and
the life, and if He can't do it He is going to get
Himself into trouble, for He said that He
could, and all the town of Bethany is full of
higher critics and every eye is on Him and it
is up to Him to do something. His bitterest
enemies were there and they watched him as a
hawk would watch a chicken. Up to that
day they had denied every claim that He had
made and rejected both Him and His doctrine,
and now He makes a claim that goes far beyond anything He has claimed up to date—
that he is the resurrection and the life. But I
believe He can do it.

CHAPTER VIII.

CHRIST INQUIRES ABOUT THE DEAD MAN.

Now we have come to the eighth stage in the history of this man Lazarus. We have just discussed the first ray of hope and Christ the resurrection and the life. The next thing that we want to notice is Christ not only in town and not only the resurrection and the life, but now he makes inquiry about the dead man. Listen to His own words. He says: "Where is he?" Now it begins to look like He meant just what He said when He said that I am the resurrection and the life. Here He is in town and He said I am the resurrection, and He said, Where is he? No doubt those old Jews said, Well, He claims to be the resurrection and the life, but He will never go to the grave of Lazarus, for they knew that Lazarus was a dead man, not a sick man,—no put on about it, for they had helped to bury him and they had been there four days weeping with Martha and Mary.

Now, mother, if Jesus comes to town and makes inquiry about your dead boy whom you know is dead in trespasses and in sins, whatever you do, never stop until you get Christ to come to the grave of your boy and call him out of the tomb of spiritual death and set him free. Christ says, Where is he, and He acts just like He wanted to find him. I believe that those old Jews began to feel a little shaky, for here is Christ right in town and Lazarus has been dead already four days. At once Christ proceeds to tell just what He can do, and He said that He could raise a dead man to life; and now He goes so far as to ask about Lazarus and says, Where is he? it really looks like He wanted to find him; but at this moment a few of those old Jews believed that something might be done. Some of them were still hard and cold and critical, and watched Him with an evil eye, and tossed their heads and said, Oh well, the Pharisees have proven Him to be an impostor, but a man of faith can begin to feel revival fire in the air, and already the people are beginning to talk meeting and some of the hardest cases in town have have been asking when the revival would start, if the revivalist had come, and if they thought he would be a success. Praise the Lord, He has come and He is a great success, and we are just as sure

to have a revival before He leaves town, as the
world stands. Glory to His name!

Just here we read that some of the Jews
went their way. Oh yes, the world is still go
ing their way, and it is an awful
way. Just think of a man turning away
from the blessed Son of God and going
his way; where will his way lead him, do you
think? Down to the pit of eternal despair, of
course. But thank God, Christ is in town, and
has already said, I am the resurrection and the
life. He has already inquired about Lazarus
and asked, Where is he? Oh, reader, if I could
have felt that Christ was inquiring about me, it
would have almost tickled me to death. To-
day there are not less than 500,000 men and
women in the United States, who, if they could
just feel that Christ loved them well enough to
inquire about them, would get saved in the next
forty-eight hours; but they are down and nobody cares for them and the devil tells them
that Christ will ruin them if they give Him their
lives; that He will rob them of all of their
pleasure and fun. While he lies on the Son
of God he doesn't tell them that he himself
has made them miserable and wretched and
hopeless and friendless and homeless. What
a vile devil he is. He tells them that God is a

hard Master and for them to never trust Him
with their lives; at the same time while he de-
ceives them he keeps them blinded to the awful
effect of sin on the human family, and while he
has broken hearts, robbed heaven, populated
hell, broken up homes, wrecked lives and dis-
graced whole communities, he is so sly and
subtle that he keeps all of this in the back-
ground.

The devil will say to a man, serve me and I
will make you a happy man, and turn around
and rob him of his manhood and swing him off
of the gallows by the neck, and put him in hell
and laugh at him as he goes down.   The other
sinners will stand by and see the whole thing
and go right on in the service of the devil.
Didn't the word of God call him a deceiver,
and a devil and a serpent and a dragon and
Satan, and the accuser of the brethren?   How
many women he has robbed of every hope and
laughed at their dying groans and mocked
them as they tried to call on God for mercy in
the jaws of death.   Yet the women are almost
as bad as men and will flirt with the world or
die, and go to an awful hell in spite of the
grace of God, and the blood of Jesus Christ
and the prayers of God's people.   And in the
face of wreck and ruin the devil will tell men

that if they will follow him he will give them freedom.

Well, I saw 1,036 the other day in one of the state prisons behind the wall with striped clothes on that the devil had set free, and I just watched them, as the overseers looked on, and wondered if they were out if they would give up sin and follow the blessed Son of God and enjoy real freedom; or would they go into sin again and get back into the pen and go on enjoying the devil's freedom. You see, the devil's freedom is a bloated face and a big stomach and a red nose and greasy breeches and run down shoes, a slouch hat, and no home, no friends, and jails and prisons and scaffolds. Doesn't that look like freedom?

CHAPTER IX.

CHRIST SEEKS THE DEAD MAN.

Dear reader, we come to the ninth stage in the history of the man Lazarus. We saw him sick, dead, bound, entombed, and putrified, and then we first saw Christ appear on the scene and declare Himself to be the resurrection and the life. Then He inquired about the dead man, and now He is seeking for the dead man. We read in Matt. 18:11: "For the Son of Man is come to save that which was lost," and again we read in Luke 19:10: "For the Son of Man is come to seek and to save that which was lost."

No person ever came on such a mission as the one that the Son of God came on. His was purely a missionary journey, and thank God it was self-supporting, for we were unable to do what He came to do, and in this narrative we have Christ in the town of Bethany, seeking a dead Lazarus. If we will lift up our eyes and behold we will not only see Him seeking a Lazarus, but we will see Him seeking a lost world. He is seeking the sinner, the wanderer.

the lost, the homeless, the friendless, the tempest-tossed, sin-sick soul. Hear His voice, take courage, and rise up, for He calleth for you, and while He seeks the sinner He does many other things. He meets a blind man and says to him, Go to the pool of Siloam and wash, and he went and washed and came seeing. He met a man with a withered hand and said to him, Stretch it out, and immediately his hand was restored whole as the other. On His journey He met up with a man that was deaf and the Lord spoke to him and the sound of the voice of the Son of God entered into his head and he never had any more trouble with his hearing. Well, I say glory to God!

He met a man with the leprosy and said to him, Go shew yourself to the priest and as he went he was cleansed from his awful disease and turned back to give glory to God. He met a man with the palsy and spoke the living word to him and the man had no more trouble with his nerves all the days of his life. I do praise the Lord that I am a believer and a shouter also. Glory to God! I am in this thing all the days of my life. Hallelujah!

We next read that He met a woman that had been diseased for twelve years and she had spent all her living on the physicians and was no better, but rather grew worse. When she saw Jesus she said, If I may but touch His garments I shall be made whole, and she slipped in behind Him and touched His garments and immediately she was made whole. I tell you, old boy, a Savior who can do that is worth tying on to. Bless His dear name. Again we read that one beautiful Sabbath morning the blessed Son of God was out for a morning stroll. He went out about the sheep market and He saw a poor man on a cot, by one of the pools of Jerusalem, who had been there for thirty-eight years. Jesus looked at him and said, Arise, take up thy bed and walk and go unto thy house, and behold, the next thing we see is a man going down the streets of Jerusalem with a bed on his shoulder. Oh my, the next thing we see is those old Jews. Now just listen to them. They say to him, It is not lawful for you to carry your bed on the Sabbath day. But listen to him. He said to them, He who made me whole said to me, Take up thy bed and walk. Bless the Lord, somebody had been to town that could do something. There that poor man lay for thirty-eight years and I don't suppose that one of those old Jews ever prayed with that poor fellow in his life, but just as soon as the blessed Son of God got him off of his bed they raised a racket with him. How much like some of the rest of us that sounds. After Jesus met us and blotted out all of our sins and called us into His blessed work and sanctified us and then healed us and put us out on the turnpike for glory; then the D. D.'s began to wherefore and whereas, and resolve and be it known that, we do not indorse or take any part with or have anything to do with the meeting that is now being held by the said ———. I will just leave off the name and you can put your name there and you will have the key to the gate.

But thank the Lord the blessed Christ went on down the stream of time and He met a poor woman with seven devils in her, cast them out, and left her rejoicing, and I suppose that Mary hasn't quit rejoicing yet. Well, I can't stand much more. I want to shout now. I know that she loved Him for we find her at the grave weeping. In His strolls through the country He met up with a few fellows fishing and He said to them, Let down your net for a draught; to their surprise they caught a boat load. Ho, man, He knows where to catch 'em, and they always bite His hook or go into His net, one or the other. He went on out into the mountain and a great multitude came out to hear Him preach and they hung on His word until they were hungry and famishing. He blessed five barley loaves and two small fishes, and fed five thousand men besides women and children. That night He wanted to cross Galilee and the boat was gone and He did something that no other man has ever done; He went afoot, and the waves of Galilee were adamant under His feet; He did not get the soles of His sandals wet.

At another time we see Him out on Galilee and an awful storm came up. He was asleep and the disciples became much alarmed and awoke Him and said, Master, we perish. He arose and rebuked the wind and the sea and they obeyed Him. Every blue breaker went back into his hole and shut his eyes and kept quiet because the Master had spoken.

When He had reached the other shore or come over to the country of the Gadarenes, He met a man with a legion of devils in him and He cast them out and the whole herd of devils ran into a herd of swine and they were choked in the sea. The last time we saw the man he was clothed and in his right mind, sitting at the feet of Jesus and wanting to become an evangelist. But the Master said to him, Go back to your house and tell what great things the Lord has done for thee. He went on his journey and found a woman at Jacob's well and told her her life's story, and caused a great revival to break out in a city of Samaria and she found that a greater One than Jacob was there. As He journeyed on in search of those who needed help He found a man up a sycamore tree and said to him, Make haste and come down, for I must abide at your house today. The man came down, and thank the Lord he got religion between the first limb and the ground, straightened up his life, and I expect to see him in heaven. Glory to God in the highest!

Now, reader, it was this same Jesus that we have been telling you about who came to Bethany and declared Himself to be the resurrection and the life, and inquired about the man Lazarus, and He is now seeking for him. I believe He will find him in spite of that old critical Jew, and in spite of the doubts of Martha and in spite of the fact that Lazarus has been dead four days already. I believe that something will be done. I can feel the victory now and hear the roar of the battle. I am expecting an old-fashioned revival to break out and shake the whole town and put the whole pit in confusion and knock the scales off of the

eyes of those old Jews and bury the doubts of
Mary so deep under the hills of Bethany that
she will never see them again in this world.
Well, amen. Keep up your faith, the victory
is ours. Christ is in town and the revival is on
and the devil is almost ready to give up the fact
that something will be done. A little faith in a
big Jesus will bring a big blessing to the heart
of any of God's children.

Now we have come to the next stage in the
history of this, the most remarkable man that
is described in the New Testament or the Old
either. Before we take up the next chapter I
want you to see just how much ground Lazarus
does cover. We first saw him a sick man;
second, we saw him a dead man; third, we saw
him a bound man; fourth, we saw him an entombed man; fifth, we saw him a putrified
man; sixth we saw Jesus appear on the scene;
seventh, we saw Jesus, the resurrection and the
life; eighth, we saw Jesus making inquiries
about the dead man; ninth, we saw Jesus seeking for the dead man, and tenth, we see Jesus at
the grave of the dead man weeping over him.
The reader will notice that there is no hope of
Lazarus in the world. If some power unknown
to man doesn't enter into him he will stay there
in that tomb forever and ever, for he is beyond

turning a new leaf, and he is beyond new resolutions and he is beyond human enthusiasm, for
he is dead and putrified and in the tomb and
the tomb is sealed up.   Without a doubt, he is
a dead man, but thank God there is hope, for
Christ is in town.

CHAPTER X.

CHRIST AT THE GRAVE.

Now, for a little while we want to look at Christ at the grave of Lazarus weeping over him. This is one of the most touching incidents in the life of the blessed Son of God. It brings out the heart and tenderness and love of the blessed Christ as no other incident that is recorded. We see Him at another time weeping over the city of Jerusalem, and as we hear Him say, Oh Jerusalem, Jerusalem, thou that killest the prophets and stones them that are sent unto thee, how oft would I have gathered thee together as a hen doth her chickens under her wings, but ye would not; therefore your house is left unto you desolate. And as He behold the city He wept over it, but at the same time it seems that when He saw the broken-hearted sisters, the criticising Jews, the doubting of the sisters of Lazarus, and knowing that they had given up all hope and that Lazarus was now a ghastly corpse in the tomb, His poor heart almost broke and he stood and wept with Mary and Martha. He said to Martha, Your brother shall rise again; and Martha said, I know that he shall rise again in the last day. She could not grasp the thought that Lazarus would rise that day.

It seems that it is much easier to have faith for the future than to have faith for the present. Martha had no trouble in believing that Lazarus would be raised at some future time, but to bring it right down to the present moment, she doubted it, and I have met with so many mothers who thought that at some future time their son would be saved and they seemed to rest in perfect ease about it. At the same time they had no faith on earth for their son at the present time, and he was just as dead and hopeless as Lazarus.

The devil comes up and helps people to have a future faith. He says, Oh well, it will all come out right in the end; go and have a good time and don't bother yourself about it. The Lord will bring it all out just right,—but he doesn't tell them that while they are going on and living without a burden for the lost that he has them in his hand and that they are just as hopeless as Lazarus. Just as truly as the blessed Son of God wept over Lazarus He is weeping over every sinner on earth to-day; and just as truly as Lazarus was dead and bound and in the tomb and putrified, every sinner in the land to-day is in the same condition morally; and just as truly as Lazarus was in a hopeless condition every sinner is in the same condition. The very fact that Christ wept over Lazarus shows us that He was interested in him, and if He was interested in Lazarus He is in every sinner in all this broad land of ours. If Lazarus was not a hopeless case then there is hope of every sinner in the land, for there is no man that could be more corrupt morally that Lazarus was physically. He was just as bad off as a fellow ever gets, and we will see pretty soon that there was hope of him. It is not any easier for the Master to raise a fellow from the dead that has only been dead one day than it is to raise one that has been dead four days. The same life-giving word that it takes to raise a man that has been dead one day would raise him if he had been dead ten years, and we see that when it comes to the salvation of a man's soul that the same act of divine grace that it takes to forgive a twelve-year-old boy will save his father. One word from the Master will settle all questions. Glory to His name.

CHAPTER XI.

THE FIRST COMMAND.

Now, reader, we have come to a very interesting fact in the history of this remarkable man. We now have the first command from the blessed Savior. It was given to the church. You will remember that the woman in the old Book most always represents the church, and we now listen to the first command. What was it? Well, just stop a minute and listen, and you will hear just what it was: "Take away the stone." If every church in the land would obey and take away the stone there would be such a revival break out, as has never been heard of since the day of pentecost.

We can look at anything that hinders a revival and it will take the place of the stone at the grave of Lazarus; one card playing Christian, one dancing Christian, one theatre going Christian can prevent and keep a revival out of a church for a whole year. A few of these kind altogether may keep a revival out for several years. But here is the Master at the grave and the tears are still on His cheeks. His voice rings out loud and clear, Take ye away the stone; but oh my, the church has got to the place where she doesn't believe in revivals and she begins to make some sort of an excuse and proceeds to tell the Master the condition of the community. Listen at the awful description of the man. Lord, by this time he stinketh.

Now reader, you have the condition of every sinner in the land until he is regenerated; but thank the Lord the Master has given His command and right in the face of the unbelievers He stands by the tomb and says, Take away the stone. Listen to His words to Martha when she was just about without a particle of faith. He said to her, Did I not say unto thee if thou wouldest believe thou shouldest see the glory of God? She believed and obeyed the Master and the stone of difficulty was removed and behold there was great joy in that city, for the revival broke out, and it always will when the church obeys the command of the Master. When we see what took place there just by obedience it looks like every church in the land would go to work at once to get all of the hindrances out of the way, for it will be impossible for the revival to break out while these things are in the way.

Every card playing and every dancing, thea-

ter going church member is a great stone that
the devil has rolled in the way of an old time
revival, and until we rise up and obey the Master's command we will never see a revival in
the church that is bound by worldliness. It is
impossible. If you will look just for a minute
you will see that it would have been impossible
for Lazarus to have ever been raised from the
dead. So it is with your own son. He is dead
and bound and entombed and putrified; the
tomb is sealed up and a great stone is rolled
against the mouth of the grave. The Master
stands without and says to us, Take away the
stone; remove all of the difficulties; get ready,
look up, and expect a revival; throw every
doubt away, pull up unbelief by the roots and
throw it over the fence; put all the faith that
you have on the throne; muster all of the courage possible, and look the world in the face and
tell them to come to the old-fashioned revival,
for it is on. Expect the altars to be full from
the first service, for the Mester is in town and
He is at the grave of Lazarus and has given
the command, Take away the stone, for the revival is on just now and somebody will be converted in the first service. That always takes
place when the church obeys the Master and
removes all the stones.

Now we want to move to the next step in this man's life, or history and see what took place when the stone was removed. It will be worth while to look at the next stage of Lazarus.

CHAPTER XII.

THE CALL OF THE MASTER.

The stone has been removed and now listen to the call of the blessed Christ, "Lazarus, come forth." And he that was dead came forth, bound hand and foot, with a napkin about his month. Reader,Lazarus as a resurrected man is one of the most beautiful types of the blessing of regeneration that can be found in the Bible. Lazarus proves that our holy religion is not man-made and proves it to be supernatural. Don't you see that Lazarus was beyond turning a new leaf? Don't you see that he was beyond a little human enthusiasm? Don't you see that he was beyond signing a card? Don't you see that it would have been impossible for him to have ever gotten out of the tomb? Don't you see that he was beyond the help of man? Even man, in all of his glory, was unable to do one thing in the world for Lazarus, for he was dead, bound, entombed, and putrified, and the tomb was sealed up and he on the inside. Ho, man, it will take a God to ever get you out of that tomb. Now Lazarus stands before us a living man, which is a type of the new birth. We saw him dead and now we see him a living man, and it is no sleight of hand performance, for it is a well known fact that he was dead and now he is alive. There he stands in the presence of the Christ.

But there is another fact that I want you to see and it is this, that while Lazarus is alive and represents the new birth, he also brings out another fact in the experience of every regenerated man. While he has life he is still bound and he has the strings on him yet. We see him a living man and he stands in the presence of the Master, and there is shouting ground and rejoicing enough for us to shout over for the next thousand years. While that is true and we all see it, at the same time he has the cords on him also, and we have seen Christians all over the land as completely bound by the opinions of other folks as Lazarus was with strings. Reader, just think of the twentieth century church and take one look at it and you will see a Lazarus standing before you completely bound. Look at the present and you will see men and women bound by a man-fearing spirit, bound by the opinions of the other fellow, bound by the cords of worldliness, bound by the awful secret oaths of their lodges,

and it is not an uncommon thing for men and
women to dance and play cards and run after
the circus, theater, and all kinds of worldliness.

Now, I want you to see that when Lazarus
got out of the tomb there was something else
that he needed.   Then take a look at the average church member and in all kindness and
honesty you are forced to say that the church
member needs the strings taken off of him as
bad as Lazarus did.   Lazarus was alive, but
he was bound.   The regenerated man is alive,
but he is bound.   Nevertheless, while we stand
and look at the Christians we wonder why they
don't walk in the light as He is in the light;
but then we remember that their feet are still
bound, fo rhis feet were bound.   We wonder why they don't clap their hands, and then
we remember their hands are still tied. Then
we wonder why they don't shout, and behold
we look and see that the napkin is still over
their mouths.   We know that a man can't do
much with a napkin over his mouth.   When
will the church get all of the strings off and
get to the place where she can walk, leap, rejoice, praise God and clap her hands, and rejoice with joy unspeakable and full of glory.

We see that the resurrected Lazarus is a
type of the new birth but we see that the bound

Lazarus is a type of the unsanctified Christian. It is life and strings and life and strings; a living man but a bound man; a living church but a bound church; a man next to helplessness and a church next to hopelessness. I know that some good people will say, Well now, Bro. Robinson, if Lazarus still had the strings on him, his conversion was not complete, and they will say that conversion is a perfect work or it is a failure one or the other. You will notice this fact, that the resurrection of Lazarus was a perfect resurrection, and also that Lazarus had perfect life, but he still had the cords on him.

You will also notice that the new birth of a Christian is a perfect birth, and that the new convert has perfect life, but Lazarus, like it, still has the strings on; so you see a perfect birth and new life in the new convert, but at times there will be cords of anger or cords of pride, or there will be cords of jealousy, or cords of the man-fearing spirit, or a craving for the things of the world, which is out of harmony with the blessed, sweet will of God. We see all of those things almost every day of our lives, as we go up and down in this country, and I have seen them by the thousands tumble into the altar and pray through and get all of the strings broken; that is the only hope of the

church to-day.   I am glad to see the man out
of the tomb, but I am so anxious to see him get
every string taken off.   I would love to live in
this country just a few years when every Christian in the United States had every cord broken
and was as free and   happy as a bird that
cleaves the blue sky.   How many Christians
have been called on to pray and at once begged
to be excused, and there was no excuse on
earth that they could offer,   only they were
bound hand and foot   and still had a napkin
about their mouth.

I know a lot of Christian folks who never
say a word of all the Lord has done for them.
Their voice is never heard.   They go to church
on Sunday if the weather will permit, but if it
rains or is too hot they sit at home all day and
the Sunday papers of course afford their liter-
true.   Not one of them ever thinks of being a
witness for the Lord.

Now, reader, I am going to show you one
of the most pitiful things in the whole land.
Well, you ask, What is it?   It is a Christian
all bound by the things of the world until they
are perfectly helpless and almost lifeless and
just about hopeless.   To see a sinner bound by
the cords of this world is sad enough, but to see
a Christian all tied up until he is a slave of the

devil is one of the saddest things I ever looked at and as you look at Lazarus you see so many confessing Christians.   Brother, there is no mistake about it, we are not deceived, we are not preaching heresy, it is an awful fact. Lazarus is a bound man; although he has life, and is in the presence of the Lord a bound man.

Not twenty-four hours ago a young man told me that his elder did not want him to preach on holiness for fear that he would dishearten the young converts.   Now reader, do you suppose that it would have disheartened Lazarus for somebody to have told him that he could get all of those strings off of his feet and hands, and that he could get that napkin off of his mouth?   How an elder can make up his mind to the awful fact that his members are better off with hands, feet and mouth bound, is a mystery to both God and man; and, I might say, to angels.   Oh, the deadness in the average church; how helpless they are no man can tell.   Think of a church with 565 members and only 15 of that number can be counted on at the prayer meeting, and only five out of the fifteen that are willing to work in the altar, and try to get sinners converted. Man, do you tell me that they are not bound?   Do you tell me that they are happy and free, and do you tell!

me that they don't need another work of grace? Why man, just look at the multiplied numbers of the leading church members who are as worldly as the sinners of your town, and you can't look at them and tell any difference in them and the sinners.

CHAPTER XIII.

THE SECOND COMMAND.

Now reader, we have come to the second command of the Savior. We have seen the first command and also the first call, but now we want to look at the second command. What was it? We will see for ourselves.

Listen to the words of Jesus as He said "Loose him, and let him go." This is the second command of the Master. The first command was, Take ye away the stone, and the second is, Loose him, and let him go. You can see the importance of this second command. How important it is that we get all of the strings off of us.

We see in these two commands the two works of grace. Notice, the first was to take away the stone; that had to be done before Christ could call Lazarus out of the tomb. After the stone was removed we hear Christ say, Lazarus, come forth, and behold we see a living man before us, and to our surprise he is still bound, hand and foot, and the napkin is still over his mouth. Now we hear Christ say

to the church, "Loose him, and let him **go.**"
This brings out the twofold mission of the
church in the world. We are to get sinners
converted and we are to get believers into the
experience of sanctification. Lazarus called out
of the tomb is the new birth, and Lazarus set
free is a type of sanctification. Everything on
earth that we are to do is hinged on the fact
that we get all of the strings off of us. No man
is at his best for God or man until he is wholly
sanctified, and of course if no man is at his best
for God, how could he be at his best for himself, or the church of which he is a member.
Therefore, I offer you this thought: If a church
that is unsanctified is left for a year or two
without a pastor it will die and you may go
back in a year or two and not find a thing of
the church left. Well, why is that? Because
a church with its hands and feet tied and a
napkin over its mouth can't feed itself and if
they don't have a pastor to look after them they
will die; but it is not so with a holiness man. I
have seen men and women all over America,
who had been without a pastor all the way
from one year to maybe a half dozen years,
and they would be standing as true as steel,
with the glory still in their souls.

Well, why is it that a sanctified man can

live better than the unsanctified?   It is because
the sanctified man has got all of the strings off
and can feed himself.   That is the reason.
Look at Lazarus bound hand and foot and
even his mouth tied.   How in the world would
you expect him to feed himself?   Don't you
see that if he doesn't get help he will die, and
now how long would a card-playing, dancing
church live without a pastor?   You can see
that they are as completely bound as Lazarus
was, and therefore they can't feed themselves.
How thankful I am that we can have every
cord broken and have perfect freedom, and because we are free we don't advocate the idea
that holiness people don't need a pastor and
don't enjoy one, for they do.   To go to church
and enjoy a message they beat any people that
it has ever been my privilege to meet.   They
enjoy the message as no other people on earth
can, from the fact that they have the use of
their hands and feet.   They can walk in the
ways of the Lord and can clap their hands for
joy; the napkin is off of their mouths and now
they can praise God with a loud voice.   Therefore, they are world beaters when it comes to
enjoying a religious service.

The crowd that is bound by the things of
the world never seems to really enjoy a relig-

ious service, and as the people with all of the
strings off leap and praise God, and clap their
hands, the bound crowd looks on with perfect
amazement.   In fact they don't see a thing in
the world to praise God for.   While the holiness crowd is just tearing up the ground the
other folks look on and wonder why these folks
are so awfully excited, when there is really
nothing to shout about.   But don't you see that
they have been called out of the tomb of spiritual death, and don't you see that they have got
every string off of them?   It is no wonder to
me that they shout. It is a wonder that they
ever keep still.

So the Master said, Loose him, and let him
go.   Yonder stands a bound man, but look
again and yonder stands a free man,—not only
out of the tomb, but out of the strings.   I have
seen people so completely bound by the opin-
ious of folks that it almost fit them like a garment; and I have seen big strong men so bound
by the man-fearing spirit that they were almost miserable and had but little religious joy
for fear they would offend somebody up town
who did not believe in making a noise.   Well,
folks, if such a fellow had been there the day
that Christ and His disciples came into Jerusalem and if they had seen the disciples leaping

and praising God and breaking down the limbs of the trees and throwing down their coats and whooping to the top of their voices, such a fellow would have had a convulsion right on the spot. Men don't have to have much religion to give God a good deal of glory and the more they have the more glory they are going to give their Lord. One of the greatest commands that ever fell from the lips of the Son of God was, Loose him and let him go, and for the past ages the church has heard His voice as He called out to His ministering servants, Loose him, and let him go.

Again, there is in the bosom of every man a longing to be perfectly free, and no man is a free man who has the carnal mind in his heart, for the carnal mind is in fact the cords that bind men. When the carnal mind is gone and the old man is destroyed then brother you are a free man, and not till then. I don't care what you may have or may not have, you are not a free man until old carnality is gone.

I heard a young man say the other day, O Lord, crucify the old man and then back up the hearse and haul off old carnality, and I said, Well, glory, that is a new one on me, but it is a good one and I will remember it.

As long as the roots of bitterness or the car-

nal mind or the old man or the body of sin are
allowed to remain there cannot be perfect freedom in the religious life; but thank God, Christ
says in a loud voice, Loose him and let him go.
Every string can be removed and the child of
God can be made as free as heaven, and we
can walk through this old world as clean as if
we were in heaven. Of course the devil doesn't
die when we get the strings off and thank the
Lord we don't either, in the sense of be
ing dead to what the devil is doing; we are
alive and we catch on to what he is up to and
we are ready to meet his assaults. With all of
the strings off and Christ enthroned in the
soul we are more than conquerors through Him
that loved us and gave Himself for us that He
might redeem us from all iniquity, and purify
us unto Himself a peculiar people, zealous of
good works.

Now, reader, when you come to think about
it, the most beautiful thing that you ever saw
was a Christian without a thing in the way of
their Christian work. Take a man or a woman
who is all given up to God and delivered from
the man-fearing spirit, who is delivered from
the people, who is long-suffering and plenteous
in mercy and filled with all the fulness of God,
who knows how to love God and lost human-

ity, how to pray and bring things to pass, you look at them and admire them because of their freedom and deliverance. You would not have the same respect for them if they were all tied up with the world. But a free man is the ideal of all men, and what makes men free? Nothing but to be delivered from all sin and filled with all the fulness of God. That means out of the tomb and all of the strings off.

CHAPTER XIV.

LAZARUS AT THE FEAST.

Now, reader, I want you to see Lazarus feasting with his Lord. That is the subject of this chapter. After Lazarus was resurrected and got the strings off of him the next thing that we see of him is at the feast. He is feasting with his Lord and Master, and it is a fact, no man ever feasts with his Lord until he is wholly sanctified. How natural it is to see a man feasting with his Lord after he gets all the strings off. You will notice that Lazarus never feasted with his Lord as long as there was a string on him, and neither do we. We must be powerfully converted and then most gloriously sanctified to feast with the Lord.

There is much connected with a feast, and the real object of a feast is to get full. I know that the linen is generally the best that can be secured in a great feast and the china is something lovely; the waiters are the best, and the food is the most appetizing that can be secured or the best that the market can afford. Just think of a black walnut table and the finest linen, the most lovely china and silver knives and forks, the most lovely teapots and well dressed waiters, and the governor of the feast giving orders and the waiters flying in every direction, but not one thing on the table to eat. Don't you think that the feast would be a flat failure? Why, of course it would, because that which goes in to make up a feast was left out, and that was the food. Don't you see that the object of a feast is to get full? The very word feast carries with it the idea of something good and plenty of it.

We see Lazarus at the feast. We read that Martha served but Lazarus was one of them who sat at the table with Him; there is no way to describe the joy and peace that comes to the life of a wholly sanctified man. About the best way to describe it is in the text, just simply feasting with your Lord, and it is called the fulness of joy. Why is it called the fulness of joy? Because it fills the man with foy and a filled man is a full man; it is also called the fulness of the blessing of the gospel of Christ; there is the same idea of being full, or the idea of a feast.

We read that Joshua, the son of Nun, was full of the spirit of wisdom; that Stephen was full of the Holy Ghost, that Barnabas was full of the Holy Ghost and of faith, and that when the day of Pentecost had fully come the disciples were all filled with the Holy Ghost. All this carries with it the idea of being full, and so we just look around and see Lazarus feasting with his Lord.   Bless his holy name, it is His plan and purpose for every one of His children to come to the feast.

On one occasion the Master said to His disciples to go out and invite the hungry multitudes to come to the feast, for all things are now ready.   The business of the church is to take away the stone and get Lazarus out of the tomb, get him wholly sanctified, get all of the strings off of him and get him to feasting with his Lord.   Who can tell the good that would come to this world if the church would go down before God and get the experience of Scriptural holiness, and truly go to feasting with her Lord.

Now, reader, it might not be out of place to just let your mind run back over the life of Lazarus for a few minutes and see what progress he has made.   The first time that we saw him, he was a sick man; the second time we saw him, he was a dead man; the third time that we saw him, he was a bound man; the fourth time we saw him he was an entombed man; the fifth

time we saw him, he was a putrified man; the sixth time we saw
him, he was a resurrected man; the
seventh time we saw him, he was resurrected
but he was still bound; the eighth time we saw
him, he was a free man—every string was off
of him, and he was as free as heaven; and the
ninth time we saw him, he was feasting with
his Lord. Now, reader, just look and see what
wonderful progress this man has made all the
way from the tomb to seat at the table with
Jesus. What a work there is for the church to
do if she was up to the place where the Lord
could use her. If she would go to work and
get the strings all off and get to the place where
she could feast with her Lord there would be
plenty of sad souls looking on who would be
ready to surrender and call on the Lord for
mercy if they could just see the church feasting
with her Lord one time.

Now in a kind way I want to just call your
attention to a church that I was in not long ago.
It was a beautiful red pressed brick that cost
nearly $75,000 and they had run for thirteen
years and had not seen a single soul brought to
God. Now don't you see that they had not
taken away the stone? Don't you see that it
was impossible for the Lord to get Lazarus out

of the tomb?   Don't you see that there was no
chance on earth for that church to ever have
a spiritual feast?   Don't you see that Lazarus
had to be called out of the tomb, and don't you
see also that Lazarus had to not only be called
out of the tomb, but he had to have the strings
all taken off of him before he could go to the
feast?   Therefore the church had stood there
all these long years without seeing a soul
brought to Christ.

To show you that church members are
bound by the things of this world I was in a
nice town in the month of October, 1908, and
there was a nice church in the beautiful city
with 588 members on the roll. One night while
I was in the town the prayer meeting was held
and there were eleven persons present; the next
night there was a church entertainment and according to the report of the town paper, there
were 1,100 out.   Now there was feasting,
but not with the Lord.   The feast of Lazarus
was a type of the spiritual life that he received
when he was called out of the tomb and when
he got the strings off of him; and the hope of
the church is to get to the place where she will
have 1,100 out to pray, sing, shout, and testify for the Lord, and let the world know that
we are free and happy, that we are going

through with Jesus, and that it is a much greater feast to serve the Lord than it is to serve the devil. It is a well known fact that sin can never produce happiness and the devil has no happy men and women. and those who serve him are unhappy, miserable, sad, and in despair and without hope; nothing but death, sorrow, hell and damnation looks them in the face; that is the reason so many of them are committing suicide and ending their own lives—they are deceived by the devil and led by him captive at his will.   But not so with the man who walks with God.

To be called out of the tomb of sin, of despair, of despondency and the tomb of death, and to stand in the presence of the Lord with spiritual life and to know for your own self that you are out of the tomb, and that new life has entered into you is blessed. Not only that, but have got all of the strings of this old world off of you, and are heaven-born, heaven-bound, heaven-filled and the glory of God is burning on the altar of your soul; that you are now ready to go to singing the lovely little song, I am feasting with my Lord, I am feasting, I am feasting on the living word.   Day by day I have a new supply, I am feasting, I am feasting with my Lord, redeemed by His blood, forgiven by His blood, and sanctified by His blood, and kept by the power of God through faith unto the end; that is, the end of our probation. We are kept here, but in heaven we will not be tempted by sin and the devil. Glory to God forever!

CHAPTER XV.

LAZARUS PERSECUTED.

The reader will notice that while Lazarus was at the feast that the chief priest laid a plot to put him to death. It is a very dangerous thing yet, in some localities, to feast with the Lord. One thing that carnality can't stand, is to see a holy man or woman really enjoy the presence of the blessed Holy Ghost. I have seen opposers just broil with anger while the true children of God were feasting with the Lord; and so we notice that it was not the the sinner, the saloon keeper, the gambler, the fighter, the dancer, the Sabbath desecrater, the man in the chain gang, the man just out on bond, nor the common people, for they heard him gladly; not the common preacher even, but just stop and take the second look. It was the chief priest, and what did this man want to do? Why, man, he went so far as to lay a plot to put Lazarus to death.

Well, what on earth was that man Lazarus doing? Just stop and look at him and see what he is doing. Behold he is feasting with his

Lord. Look out there, man, don't you shout
too loud; don't break the limbs off of that tree;
don't throw down your old coat for the Master
to ride on; you will get into an awful fix there.
You must understand, old boy, that you are
not in a political meeting. The Democrats or
the Republicans can shout as loud as they
please. The meeting that you see is not a week
of Elks. When the Elks come to town, they
can bring harlots, or they can bring whiskey or
beer right into a prohibition town and nobody
says a word, but the meeting that we refer to
is a meeting of a different kind. At this meeting we are to give the God of heaven all the
glory, praises and honor, for Thou art worthy,
O Lord God, of honor and power and glory
forever and ever. But see the frown on the
face of the chief priest. See how sullen he
looks. You would imagine that some awful
crime had been committed and the visitors in
the conference room look on and wonder what
this man has done. To their surprise they find
out that the man has gone to a holiness camp
meeting and heard of full salvation and that he
went forward and fell in the straw and was
wholly sanctified; for the last few months he
has been feasting with his Lord. Just look, you
can see two or three men in little groups all over

the conference floor and they seem to be uneasy and they tiptoe and whisper one to another; while all of this is going on you can see Lazarus sitting down over there in the corner with a smile on his face and the crowd seems to be wondering what is to become of him. There he sits with full salvation hung up all over his face and he is the only easy man in the conference. Not a wave of trouble rolls across his peaceful breast, and he says,

How well I remember in sorrow's dark night,
The lamp of His word shed its beautiful light;
More grace He has given and burdens re-
     moved,
And over and over His goodness I proved.
Shall I turn back into the world?
     Oh, no, not I, not I."

As he remembered the day that he was converted and how that he passed from death unto life, how the Lord called him out of the tomb of despair and spoke peace to his troubled soul and that his name was written in the Lamb's book of life, and that he was adopted into the heavenly family, a thrill of joy goes through his soul and he praises God for the knowledge of sins forgiven. Then he remembers the day that he put himself on the altar—soul, mind, and body for time and eternity, and how the fire from the skies went through his heart. He knew by the witness in his own breast that he was sanctified through and through and the glory rolls up and down in his heart. He is feasting with his Lord in the truest sense.

Now the chief priest is ready. Ready to do what? To locate this man. Well, what has he done? He got sanctified. What else did he do? He shouted and praised God with a loud voice. And what else did he do? He told the people everywhere he went that they could get the blessing of Scriptural holiness. Well, did he do anything else? Yes, he had revivals all over his work and built a new church or two, added a large list of new members to the roll of his church and brought up his conference collecteions in full; but he did preach holiness as straight as a gun barrel. He is to be located on the charge of inefficiency. You see he got the strings all off and went to feasting with his Lord, and that is a dangerous thing to do. Why didn't he let holiness alone? If he had joined the lodge it would have been all right, but instead of that he went to a holiness revival and got the fulness of the blessing and went to feasting with

his Lord, and trouble broke out before Lazarus
got away from the supper table.

How much like our day is this fact before
us. Reader, just let your mind run back over
the past twenty years and just think of all the
plots that have been laid and planned to keep
holiness out of the churches in the United
States of America. I heard a pastor one time
my own self in trying to keep any of his members from testifying to the experience of sanctification, tell them that in the testimony meeting
he did not want them to testify to anything that
they themselves had, but to testify on something
else. You say that was not hard. Well, I
know it wasn't, but the thing I am after is this,
there was the pastor of the flock plotting to
keep holiness out of his church, and to do just
what the chief priest did to Lazarus. The
chief priest laid a plot and God saw it and was
not well pleased with it. The hope of any
church on earth is the holiness that is in it and
not the worldliness that is in it.

I believe there is enough holiness in any
church to leaven the whole lump if the leaven
was allowed to work. If the holiness revival
that was started under that mighty man of God,
John S. Inskip, could have run on
without a break, it would have swept the

United States before now. Every time that it
has been hindered from taking the country the
chief priest was on hand, and I don't mean that
it was always a bishop or an elder. I have
known other churches to have a revival started
and those in authority would rise up and stamp
it out and stop the fire and keep their members
from seeking and obtaining the greatest thing
in the world, which is the baptism with the
Holy Ghost.

Now, reader, Lazarus a free man is a beautiful type of a wholly sanctified man, and the
persecution that broke out at the feast is nothing
uncommon, for the rulers in all ages, so far as
I have ever been able to find out, have been on
the opposite side of deep spirituality. As a gen-
eral thing a man is not big enough to stand the
prestige of an office and keep up spirituality at
the same time. No doubt that was the trouble
with the chief priest. He might have started
out well, been kind to the men under him, but
day by day his love and kindness go and he
becomes very hard, and finally reaches the
point where he is going to have his own way
if he has to take the heads off of men. The
case in hand will prove it to be true, for as far
as we can see, Lazarus had done nothing to the
chief priest, but Lazarus had been raised from

the dead, and so has the justified man; Lazarus had been set free, and so has the sanctified man; Lazarus was feasting with his Lord, and so is the sanctified man; while Lazarus was feasting with his Lord the plan was laid to dispose of him, and so it was of me, if the reader will pardon me for referring to myself.

We have said in this chapter before that one thing that old carnality can't stand is religious joy; the old man can stand all of the average church work and he is real friendly to a cold, dead formality, and will even help support a great popular revival and give freely of his means to carry on such a work, but just let the saints go to rejoicing, and the same trouble that the chief priest had in his heart will rise up today and demand of you and if you don't stop you are at least liable to get into trouble with him. There are no doubts in my mind but that there are in the United States many thousands of good people who don't know just what to do. They love their church and live right in the church, yet have but little church fellowship and they feel that they are in the way. If they rejoice in the Lord there is a very critical eye on them and they don't know just whether to give up and quiet down or go ahead and take the consequences. I am of he opinion that

Lazarus went ahead, from what followed, for the next time we see him he was a great soul winner. If he had gone back on the Lord we never would have heard of a revival from him; but thank the Lord he stood true and God was with him and the world has not quit talking about him yet.

I am to-day in love with the Lord and all mankind, and it is remarkable how the Lord has walked with me and led me by His hand. What He will do for one He will for all, and so far as I know every man will have a part in the trials and misrepresentations, and just as true as Lazarus had his trials to meet we have ours. If they don't come from one source they will come from another. It doesn't hinder the spiritual progress of the church for the devil to make an attack on us but when we as the people of God rise up in our own ranks and put on the breaks and clog the wheels of Zion, then the harm is done, and then a gulf stream of worldliness will break in on us, and it is a fact if we don't grow we will die; if we don't keep hot we will freee; if we don't keep going we will stagnate. We are like the bicycle, the faster we run the straighter we stand; the slower we go the worse we wobble, and when we stop we fall.

The hope of the world is that the church may rise up in her God-given power and get the man out of the tomb. We must rescue the perishing; the hope of the church is that as a church we may go down before the Lord and get every string taken off and be set free and then go to the feast with the Master. It makes my heart rejoice when I read that Lazarus was one of those who sat at the table with Him. Reader, let's not let anything in the world stop us. It is a fact that the chief priest did not kill him for we see him after the feast in a great revival and many believed.

CHAPTER XVI.

LAZARUS, THE SOUL WINNER.

We have come to the last chapter, and in this chapter we want to talk about winning souls. The old prophet said, He that winneth souls is wise. And again we read, And they that be wise shall shine as the brightness of the firmament, and they that turn many to righteousness, as the stars forever and ever. Again the blessed Christ said, I will make you fishers of men. At another time He said to them, Henceforth ye shall catch men. Again He said to them, Go ye into all the world and preach the gospel to every creature, and he that believeth and is baptized shall be saved, and he that believeth not shall be damned. We could go on and pile up many Scriptures, but there is no use of it.

The text for this chapter is John 12:10, 11: "But the chief priests consulted that they might put Lazarus also to death; because that by reason of him many of the Jews went away and believed on Jesus." The reader will notice that the first time we saw Laarus he was a sick man, but the last glimpse that we had of him he was a soul winner. Notice, it says that many of the Jews went away and believed on Jesus because of Lazarus; we don't know how many, but we do know that a great multitude did believe. It is a very strange thing when we think of where the Lord goes to get his preachers. How natural it was in the prophet when he went to the house of Jesse to anoint a king for the Lord. Jesse and the prophet both looked on the fine looking young men and one by one they passed before the prophet but the Spirit said, He is the one, and when all of the fine looking ones had passed and no one had been chosen, the prophet asked, Is this all of your sons? Well, Jesse said, all but one stripling who is out with a herd of sheep. The Lord had found a great preacher out with a herd of sheep once before that, and so Jesse had the lad brought and he proved to be the one. He turned out to be the sweet singer of Israel, and afterwards wrote the Twenty-third Psalm, which has brought joy and gladness to the hearts of thousands of the Lord's little ones.

To look at Lazarus as we have seen him in the different stages of death he looks like everything on earth but a revivalist; but look at the great crowd who believed on Jesus because of

Lazarus, and you will be fully persuaded in your mind that he was one of the greatest witnesses Jesus ever put on the witness stand. All Lazarus had to do was to go and tell his experience, and he stopped the mouth of all gainsayers.

Christ said one day to His disciples that I will give you a mouth and a wisdom which all of your adversaries shall not be able to resist or to gainsay. Without a doubt Lazarus had this mouth and this wisdom, for he had come from the bottom and he was on top, and the Jews knew that Lazarus was no sleight of hand performance for they had been there to the funeral and they saw Lazarus go down into the tomb a dead man. They staid there with his heart-broken sisters for the full four days and after Lazarus had been dead four days Jesus, the very one that the Jews did not like, came to town and declared Himself to be the resurrection and the life; they were right there when the Son of God called Lazarus out of the tomb. Now look at that dead man in the tomb all covered with putrefaction and just think of that man as a great revivalist. Who on earth would think of such a thing.

You will bear me witness that when Jesus went to town there was not a man in town that

had any thought on earth that Lazarus would
ever be a preacher.   Why. man, he was dead
and bound and in the tomb; he was already
putrified and the tomb was already sealed up.
Even his own nearest friends had lost all hope
and so it is to-day, but when the Lord comes to
town, and before we hardly know it, He has
the fellow out of the tomb; the next thing we
know he has all of the strings off of him; the
next thing we know he is feasting with his
Lord; the next thing we know he is persecuted,
and the next thing we know he is a great soul
winner, attracting more attention than any man
in the field.   The devil has mud on his horns
and the smoke is flying.   The devil is making
an awful howl and the chief priest says it will
never do to allow this fellow to go on in this
way.   He is out of the natural order.   O, yes,
my brother, he is out of the natural order.   He
is out of the tomb instead of being out of the
university. He is a Christ-made man, a heaven-
born man, a Spirit-filled man and as he feasted
with his Lord, the wise   looked   wise and
scratched their heads and said, He is a great
disturber of the peace of our Zion.   But the
revival is on, the altars are full, the saints are
shouting for joy, the face of Lazarus is all lit up
with the glory of God, he is all out and out for

God and the calls are coming in from all points of the compass.

The chief priest consulted that Lazarus might be put to death also, and they met, just as I have known them to do, and wrote out a long document in which they said, Be it resolved, whereas, we the undersigned have nothing to do with the meetings that are now being held in the city. I have seen wagon loads of just such as the above, and while the dear brethren were taking no stock in the holiness meeting, I want you to see that the holiness meeting did not take any stock in them. We know that real Bible holiness is the hope of the church, and when a man gets to the place that he will have nothing to do with holiness he is on awfully dangerous ground at the very best construction you can put on him and his conduct. We have a holy God and a holy Christ, the Holy Ghost and the Holy Bible, and a holy church was started by our heavenly Father. The holy apostles were left in charge of it and the object of a holy church is to make men holy. We have the holy angels to watch over us while we live holy lives, and then we are to go to a holy heaven, and live with the holy saints forever and ever. Amen and amen.

It is not hard for a holy man to have revivals

of religion anywhere on earth he goes; in fact,
the revival is on when he takes charge of the
church. I will give you a case that came under
my own observation. There were two men in
the same conference and there was but little
difference in their ages. There was no difference in their preaching ability, so far as we
could see. If there was, the one that refused
to preach holiness had the advantage of the
other. They took two churches at the same
time and were only about fifty miles apart.
There was no difference in the strength of the
two churches—just about the same. One man
had the experience of holiness and preached it
and the other did not, but fought it; the one
that preached it, in the four years, had from
two to three big revivals each year. The other
fellow did not have a revival in the four years.
The one that was all out for God and full salvation added to the church in the four years
about 400 members and the fellow that fought
holiness added one member to his church roll
in four years. The one member he got was
converted under my preaching up town in an
old storehouse meeting, and if the brother had
a soul saved in the four years nobody ever
heard of it. He was a nice man and was not a
sinner; he seemed to have some religion, and

was a good preacher. In many respects he was
a fine man, and was a friend of mine, but he
spent much time in proving to the poor hungry
multitudes that they could not be sanctified. At
a glance we see that he was not a soul winner.
He was not like Lazarus. You can read between the lines that many of the Gentiles did
not believe on Jesus because of this man, but
we see that many of the Jews did believe on Jesus because of Lazarus.

One of the greatest gifts on earth is the gift
of soul winning. How it fills my heart to hear
a man or a woman preach the gospel and fill
the altar; to see the penitents weep their way to
the altar, pray through, strike fire, and get up
with a shine on their faces and tell the glad
story of pardoning love; and at the same altar
service I love to see a number of seekers for the
blessing of sanctification; to see them get up
with the glory of God all over their souls, and
see the glory shining through their faces, and
listen to their testimony as they try to tell between their sobs and shouts, what the Lord has
done for them. Oh, it is beautiful!

I know it almost tickled Lazarus to death
just to listen to the testimonies of the people
around the town of Bethany. The high priest
was mad and Lazarus was glad, but the revival

was on; a revival of old time power is too big for the chief priest or anybody else to stop. A soul winner in a great revival is about the happiest mortal on earth and cares about as little for the growls of the chief priest as any other mortal above ground.

I see three things in the great holiness revival that I would call three gets : You have to get the blessing or get out of the way or you will get run over. Well, remember that many of the Jews believed on Jesus because of Lazarus.

www.ingramcontent.com/pod-product-compliance
Lightning Source LLC
Chambersburg PA
CBHW021202020426
42331CB00003B/169